William Watson Stockwell

New Songs and Poems for the Camp and Fireside

William Watson Stockwell

New Songs and Poems for the Camp and Fireside

ISBN/EAN: 9783337256937

Printed in Europe, USA, Canada, Australia, Japan

Cover: Foto ©Thomas Meinert / pixelio.de

More available books at **www.hansebooks.com**

AND POE

FOR THE

CAMP AND FIRE

BY WILLIAM W. STOCKW

Scorn not to read this little Book,
Though by a stranger penn'd,
For if you read it through with car
You'll be the Author's Friend;
Yes, read it through and you will fi
In style and language new,
Most cheering thoughts for all mank
And these will gladden you.

VIETS & SAVAGE,
BOOK, JOB AND CHROMOTYPE PRINTERS,
CLEVELAND, OHIO:
1864.

CONTENTS.

—o—

PREFACE.

The Songs and Poems comprising this collecti
with but two or three exceptions, have been writ
since the commencement of the present Slaveholde
Rebellion, and many of them were suggested by
citing incidents connected with the war for its s
pression.

As it has not been the fortune of the author to se
his country as a soldier, he has not written sentime
and songs for the soldier from what he has experienc
except so far as a sympathetic nature and an exci
fancy have enabled him to see and feel as the sold
sees and feels, and if he has failed in any instance
express the true sentiments of the soldier, it must
attributed alone to this fact.

Although some of the Songs and Poems will
specially interesting to the soldier, and others to
members of the soldier's home, it is believed that
citizen and general reader will be interested in all.

That this offering may go forth to cheer the soldi
and the loyal hearts of every home, and also be
means of inspiring all to labor with renewed zeal
bring the time

"When man to man united,
And every wrong thing righted,
The whole world shall be lighted
As Eden was was of old."

is the sincere wish of

THE AUTHOR

THE SOLDIER'S GOOD-NIGHT SONG.

ı͏R.—The Light Canoe, or Lake of the Dismal Swamp

come, let us join in a song, brave boys,
   As we sit by our fire's dim light;
ɛt us sing of our days of most innocent joys,
nd banish from mind every thought which destroys
   The peace of the soldier at night.

es, yes, brave boys, let us sing to-night
   Of the days when most happy were we,
the home where fond parents could gladden our sight,
nd brothers and sisters made time, in its flight,
   Gaily ring with their laughter and glee.

ıose days to us were most blissful days—
   The happiest days of our life!
e spent all the hours in the merriest ways,
ur labors were pleasant, and pleasant our plays,
   And our country was free from strife.

days of childhood and youth now flown,
   How blest do they seem in review!
ıough the present a shadow has over them thrown,
ıey seem far the brightest we ever have known,
   For the world and all hearts were then true!

ɛs, oft let us muse on those days, brave boys,
   As embathed in our life's morning dew,
ɔr theirs is a freshness time never destroys,
freshness and beauty that never cloys,
   Though oft they are held in review.

And let us muse on the future, too,
 As in hope it is pictured most fair;
And let us take heart trying scenes to go through,
Till we finish the work we are missioned to do,
 Ere the pleasures of home we can share.

And now let us go to our rest, brave boys,
 And say to the world good-night;
We will hasten then to our dreamland joys,
And forget all the world with its bustle and noise,
 Till the dawn of the morning's light.

THE SOLDIER'S SECOND DEPARTURE

A FAREWELL SONG.

Air.—*The Graves of a Household.*

Once more with firm and manly tread
 Our brother leaves his home,
To aid his comrades on the field
 When days of trial come;
Once more we bid the soldier go:
 Our fears we may not tell:
We parted once—we met—and now
 Once more we say farewell.

I look upon his youthful brow,
 Then down into his heart.
And wonder if he will be true,
 And act a manly part,

When on the field he meets the foe,
　Where balls like hail shall fly,
And fearful clouds of battle smoke
　Shall darken all the sky!

I look into his earnest heart,
　And read it o'er again,
And with each heart-throb feelings start,
　Akin to joy and pain;
I look into his very soul,
　I read it through and through,
And in my country's darkest hour
　I know he will be true.

He looks upon our country's foes
　With mercy in his eye,
He would that on the battle-field
　No more brave men might die :
He would that *words*, not guns and swords,
　Might end this fearful war,
And make all those who have rebelled
　Obey our country's law.

And, though he looks upon our foes
　With mercy in his eye,
He would have freedom's cause prevail
　Though more brave men must die !
The soldier goes to conquer foes :
　Our fears we may not tell :
We parted once—we met—and now
　Once more we say farewell.

THE SOLDIER'S FRIEND.

Oh! who is not the soldier's friend?
  Who loves not him who dares to go,
His country's honor to defend,
  And battle a rebellious foe?

His path is one of trials sore,
  And, such great dangers round it lie,
He needs of strength a lasting store
  To pass through all the scenes which try.

Far from his own loved friends and home,
  And all the social joys they know,
From place to place he's doomed to roam,
  And guard against a fearful foe.

It is the same when light and dark—
  The same 'neath clear and cloudy skies:
He is to every foe a mark,
  And danger ever round him lies.

He starts with every dawn of light,
  Upon his long day's toil and tramp,
And often takes his rest at night
  Upon a bed both cold and damp.

All hours to him are trying hours;
  They slowly wear away his life;
For storms and sunshine try his powers,
  As well as march and battle's strife.

His precious moments may be spent
  In battle—marching—out on guard,
Or lonely lying in his tent,
  But all to him is service hard.

O ! who loves not the soldier true ?
    Who loves not him who's pledged to live
His country's foemen to subdue,
    Or in the strife his own life to give ?

MISUNDERSTANDING.

Misunderstanding works no good,
    But works a world of ills :
It breaks the bonds of brotherhood,
    And warmest friendship chills.

It keeps the heart unreconciled
    As long as under ban ;
It makes the most unhappy child,
    It makes the jealous man.

It sows the fruitful seeds of hate,
    The human heart within ;
It makes of trifles troubles great,
    And thus leads man to sin.

Quite seldom men would disagree
    If they were understood ;
And if they did, it e'er would be
    Like brothers kind and good.

Then let us all be understood,
    And aim the truth to see ;
And let us seek each other's good,
    Wherever we may be.

Thus we may end time's bitter strife, .
  And live a life of bliss,
For man may live a blissful life,
  E'en in a world like this.

BROTHER AND SOLDIER.

A SONG DEDICATED TO THE SISTERS OF THE SOLDIER'S HO?

AIR.—*Listen to the Mocking-Bird.*

I'm thinking now of brother, my brother, your broth
  I'm thinking now of brother,
Who has joined our country's valiant soldier ban(
He's left sisters and mother, his mother, my mother
  He's left sisters and mother,
But he's gone to seek the welfare of our land.

Chorus.—Now in fancy oft we roam,
  From the soldier's own loved home ;
  And in our earnest songs and prayers we cra.
  Blessings on each heart and hand
  Of each valiant soldier band,
  That dares to strike for freedom or a grave.

We fancy now he's drilling, he's drilling, he's drilli
  We fancy now he's drilling,
With his noble comrades on the tented field ;
And martial strains most thrilling, most thrilling, m
  And martial strains most thrilling,   [thrilli
Fire him with an earnest zeal his arms to wield.
Chorus.—Yes, in fancy thus we roam, etc.

d scenes most dark and trying, most trying, most try-
 Mid scenes most dark and trying,   [ing,
We now seem to see him on the battle plain ;
ıd now our foes seem flying, seem flying, seem flying,
 And now our foes seem flying,
From the conflict field where lie their gory slain.
ʟorus.—Yes, in fancy thus we roam, etc.

ır household fire is burning, is burning, is burning,
 Our household fire is burning,
But before it is au ever vacant chair ;
ıd oft our thoughts are turning, are turning are turn-
 And oft our thoughts are turning,   [ing,
Southward where our brother has a soldier's fare.
ʟorus.—Yes, in fancy oft we roam, etc.

ı ! well do I remember, remember, remember,
 Ah ! well do I remember,
How the moments of his hour for parting sped—
lm as in mild September, September, September,
 Calm as in mild September,
Rose the pale moon o'er us when "good-bye" we said.
ʟorus.—Now in fancy oft we roam, etc.

other, we long to greet thee, to greet thee, to greet
 Brother, we long to greet thee,   [thee,
But if we may never meet again in time,
e hope and trust we'll meet thee, we'll meet thee, we'll
 We hope and trust we'll meet thee, [meet thee,
In eternity's divinely radiant clime.
ʟorus.—Yes, our brother, ever dear,
 If we may not meet thee here,
 Where thou wouldst give thy life our land to save,
 We would meet thee in that clime,
 Just beyond the shores of time,
Where only meet the ever true and brave.

THE SOLDIER'S MESSAGE.

Air.—*Jamie's on the Stormy Sea.*

Blow, ye south winds, northward over,
Till a home you shall discover
Where is missed a fond home-lover,
   And this message bear with thee :
Tell the loved ones there abiding,
Those in whom my soul's confiding,
Those who are home-joys providing,
   I am longing them to see.

Tell them still their love I treasure,
Thoughts of them have given me pleasure,
And in every hour of leisure
   I have longed to be at home ;
Tell them all their kind words cheer me,
Make me love my home more dearly,
Make my way of life less dreary,
   As from place to place I roam.

Tell them for their good I'm scheming,
And in hope the future's gleaming—
Tell them too I'm nightly dreaming
   Of most happy days to come ;
Yes, tell mother, wife and sisters,
In as soft as angel whispers,
How in some most sweet siestas,
   I have dreamed of them and home.

But you need not tell my trouble,
Trouble told is often double,
Raise not e'en one sorrow-bubble,
   On their life-sea to repose :

No, tell not my soul's afflictions,
Tell them not of joy's restrictions,
They have strong enough convictions
   That the soldier sorrow knows.

Tell them well my toil I'm bearing,
And though all our work is wearing,
Nothing can prevent our sharing
   Pleasure from Hope's promised joys;
So of Hope we freely borrow
Sweet relief from care and sorrow,
And each sad thought of to-morrow,
   Which the soul's true peace destroys.

Ask they further how I'm living,
Ask they of my joy and grieving—
How the future I'm receiving,
   This is all I bid you say:
Like a soldier, not the peasant;
In the future, not the present;
He is living to make pleasant
   That dear spot where home-friends stay.

Blow, ye south winds, northward over,
Till that home you shall discover,
Where is missed a fond home-lover,
   And this message bear with thee;
Then before the light of morning
Shall again be earth adorning,
Or to rise we hear our warning,
   Bear a message back to me.

THE SOLDIER'S DREAM.

AIR.—*Shed not one Tear for Me, Mother.*

I had a dream last night, dear wife,
    A dream of home and thee,
And of a change come o'er our land
    Such as I long to see.

I dreamed the war was o'er, dear wife,
    And I went home to thee,
And our beloved little ones
    I've longed so much to see.

When first into my home I stepped
    The children seemed afraid,
They did not know their father fond
    In warlike garb arrayed.

But scarce a moment passed, dear wife,
    Ere they their father knew,
And then with hearts most wild with joy
    Into my arms they flew.

Yes, they were truly happy then,
    Joy sparkled in each eye,
And so lit every face I know
    A child's face will not lie.

We talked about the war, dear wife,
    And all sad scenes passed through,
And as we to the future looked
    The world seemed fair to view.

Yet there were some dark spots beheld
  Where war its blight had left,
And we were pained to see the grief
  Of those of friends bereft.

We talked of many cherished plans
  To bless our quiet home,
And thought how happy we might live
  Through all the years to come.

We talked of peace, and peaceful ways
  To cheer and bless mankind,
And thought with lessons we had learned
  To comfort every mind.

We were most happy then, dear wife,
  Our land from strife was free,
And blest with happiness and peace,
  It seemed we e'er might be.

But morning came at last, dear wife,
  The saddest I have known,
For from this sweet dream I was called,
  To find these home-joys flown.

And now with earnest heart, dear wife,
  To keep our country free,
I turn to do the work of war,
  And then go home to thee.

THE TRAITOR'S FATE.

AIR.—*Bruce's Address.*

What will be the traitor's fate ?
What great doom doth on him wait ?
Is it more than country's hate—
    More than death to be ?
Can long years wash out the stain,
Which is on his soul and brain ?
Will his soul be free from pain,
    When across time's sea ?

'Tis a fate no mortal craves—
Worse than doom of time's worst slaves—
Worse than sinking 'neath the waves
    Of oblivion's sea !
Judas-like he longs to rise,
Judas-like he truth denies,
Judas-like he lives and dies,
    Lost in infamy !

'Tis the worst fate time can bring :
'Tis the soul's worst conscience-sting,
Barbed with scorn which true hearts fling
    Most disdainfully !
'Tis, indeed, a fearful doom,
'Tis far worse than prison gloom,
'Tis a fate worse than the tomb,
    Though it friendless be.

OUR LAND.

AIR.—*O, Susana.*

A glorious land our land will be
  When this dread war shall end,
If north and south alike are free,
  And each to each is friend ;
For time will then war's blight arrest,
  Peace her new reign begin,
And our whole country be more blest
  Than it has ever been !
Chorus.—Oh! a glorious land,
       This land of ours will be,
     When north and south united stand,
     And both are truly free !

Yes, this fair land of ours will be,
  The noblest 'neath the sun
If we are true to liberty
  Till lasting peace is won ;
For where affliction's clouds now rest,
  Will shine the light of peace,
And north and south, and east and west,
  In happiness increase.
Chorus.—Oh! a glorious land, etc.

O ! Peace, with longing hearts we turn
  Thy first fair dawn to view,
When all oppressive power shall spurn,
  And live to freedom true :
Come, bring new light to cheer all eyes,
  That all the truth may see,
And may we be more truly wise,
  To keep our country free!

Chorus.—Oh! a glorious land,
　　This land of ours will be,
　　When north and south united stand,
　　And both are truly free!

WE LOVE LIBERTY.

Air.—*O! come, come away.*

We love liberty, glad hearts to-day are singing!
　And echoes sweet the strain repeat,
　　　We love liberty!
On every northern hill and plain,
And southward where still clanks the chain,
Rings out the joyous strain,
　　　We love liberty!

We love liberty, the joyous birds are singing!
　In bush and brake the echoes wake,
　　　We love liberty!
It is the sweet song of the sea,
It is the river's chiming glee,
And sing the breezes free,
　　　We love liberty!

We love liberty, the captive soul is singing!
　No guard or chain can check the strain,
　　　We love liberty!
Although the body wears a chain,
And feels affliction's keenest pain,
The soul will breathe the strain,
　　　We love liberty!

We love liberty, both bond and free are singing!
  And echoes plain repeat the strain,
          We love liberty!
Sweet words like these our lives control,
In every heart their echoes roll,
For there lives not a soul,
          But loves liberty!

EARNEST PEOPLE.

We're a very earnest people,
  Whether jovial or sad;
We're in earnest when we're friendly,
  And in earnest when we're "mad."

· We're in earnest when we labor,
  Be our motives good or bad;
We're in earnest working ruin,
  And in making others glad.

We are earnest in our thinking,
  And the words we write are strong;
We are earnest in our talking,
  And in earnest in our song.

We are earnest in our loving,
  We're decided in our hate,
And as candid in forgiving
  As could be decreed by Fate.

We are earnest in our greetings
   When we take another's hand ;
We're in earnest loving freedom,
   And in loving freedom's land.

We are earnest in our friendship
   To all nations of the earth,
Whether kingdoms or republics,
   And we prize them for their worth.

We're a very earnest people,
   And as we in life proceed,
'Tis the height of our ambition,
   Other nations all to lead.

Every art and every science
   We are bound to understand,
And we'll use them for improvement,
   In this great and glorious land.

We are earnest and ambitious
   To make all earth's children glad,
And we're bound to be respected
   If respect is to be had.

We're a very earnest people,
   And we're bound we will be free,
And see human rights respected
   O'er our land from sea to sea.

NATIONAL SONG.

Lo, the world is on progressing!
Armed with truth for wrongs redressing,
Armies vast are forward pressing,
 With a bold and fearless tread!
All in life new steps are taking,
All the *free* are progress making,
Light on all the world is breaking,
 God is reigning overhead!

Chorus.—Yes, we're moving as a nation,
 Moving on in every station,
 For our country's preservation,
  And the cause of liberty:
 Every day the past reviewing,
 Every day our toil renewing,
 Every day some wrong subduing,
  We are growing strong and free!

As with hopes and aims far-sighted
Our forefathers here united,
And the lamp of freedom lighted,
 We will keep their lamp in trim;
Our whole country we will cherish,
All the arts of peace we'll nourish,
Nothing good shall ever perish,
 Freedom's holy light to dim!
Chorus.—We are moving as a nation, etc.

Patriot hearts, of high endeavor,
Beat as warmly now as ever,
And their sway shall lessen never,
 In this land of liberty:

Foes with threats may seek to awe us,
And with fearful weapons war us,
But with God and angels for us,
    We shall keep our country free!
Chorus.—We are moving as a nation, etc.

THE PARADISE BIRD.

Behold! o'er the earth's vast dominions
    Where no missiles of war should be hurled,
The Paradise Bird on tired pinions
    Looks down on a war-making world!
The earth is so blood-stained and dreary,
    As it comes to her piercing eye's view,
Though her pinions are ever so weary,
    She must still keep her course in heaven's blue

O! bird of that life-land elysian
    Why thus on thy weary wings fly?
Art thou sent on some glorious mission,
    Which joy to our world would supply?
Why is it that emblem thou bearest,
    Like a banner unrolled in the sky— .
An emblem more fair than earth's fairest,
    Which gladdens and wins every eye?

But what is the glorious mission
    On which thou hast earthward now flown?
Is it not to fire men with ambition,
    Such as mortals have never yet known?
Is it not to direct the attention,
    Of mortals engaged in fierce strife,
And inspire them to end their dissension,
    And live a more glorious life?

Is it not to assure all the living,
    That contention and warfare are wrong,
And that only the *true and forgiving*,
    To heaven's kingdom can ever belong?
Thy mission must surely be holy,
    Or that emblem thou never couldst bear—
It must be to inspire the earth's lowly,
    To live for a world heavenly fair.

As I gaze on thy beautiful pinions,
    As they bear thee along in the blue,
Then look on earth's blood-stained dominions,
    My soul is made sad by the view;
But fly till thy mission is ended,
    Till on earth thou canst fold up thy wings,
And where mortals too long have contended,
    Hear the songs which the peace-angel sings.

THE DYING SOLDIER'S FAREWELL.

Air.—*The Dying Californian.*

Brother Soldier, come beside me,
    Come and hear what I would say,
I would leave with thee a message,
    For my home-friends far away.

Tell them how, in this day's conflict,
    Freedom's foes I battled well,
Till most faint and weak with bleeding
    Of a mortal wound I fell.

Tell them, like a worthy soldier,
  I have aimed my task to do.
For much less will grieve my mother,
  If she knows I have been true.

As she taught me to be faithful
  In whatever I might do,
I would have her know I've ever
  To her cherished wish been true.

Tell her I have ne'er regretted
  That my home and friends I left,
To become the nation's soldier,
  Though of all home-joys bereft.

Tell her still I love my country—
  Love her laws and liberty,
And while human hearts are beating,
  I would have my country free.

To secure true peace and freedom
  On this soil my life I give,
And could I my life live over,
  For the same great end I'd live.

I shall leave a mound to freedom,
  That will ever sacred be,
Though no tears the spot may moisten,
  And no friend the spot may see.

Tell my loved ones I would meet them
  Here on earth before I die,
For to meet them and to greet them
  Would a world of joy supply.

But the distance which now parts us,
   Tells me plainly, o'er and o'er,
Though we love however fondly,
   We can meet on earth no more.

But we shall not long be parted,
   For each one fast older grows,
And the forms of all the living,
   Like my own, will soon repose.

Farewell, now, but not forever:
   Farewell till we pass from time,
And our souls enjoy a meeting
   In eternity's fair clime.

THE BANNER OF RED, WHITE AND BLUE.

AIR.—*Columbia, the Gem of the Ocean.*

Behold! o'er each land, sea and ocean,
   Proud banners float high in the air,
And hearts full of patriot devotion,
   These banners triumphantly bear;
Yes, true-hearted landsmen and seamen
   To all of these emblems are true,
But the pride of Columbia's freemen
   Is the banner of red, white and blue.

This banner our fathers defended,
  When freedom was won for our land,
And we, unto whom it's descended,
  Should be true as its guardian band.
Let us ever defend it as brothers,
  My countrymen earnest and true,
To wave o'er our sisters and mothers,
  Who cherish the red, white and blue.

'Tis the flag for the free hand's defending;
  It cheers the Columbian's eye;
And while stars gem the blue o'er us bending,
  May no star from its cherished folds fly!
The stars which are planted in heaven,
  Float ever in ether of blue,
And the stars of our banner were given,
  To *remain* in this color most true.

Thy banner, Columbia, forever,
  The stars and the stripes may it ever be,
And wave o'er a people who never
  Will bend to oppression the knee!
May the sons to whom freedom was given,
  To the cause of their fathers prove true,
And while loving the sainted in Heaven,
  Guard the banner of red, white and blue,

A DIRGE.

Air.—*Ellsworth's Funeral.*

Hark! to the tread of our soldiers,
  As slowly they pace o'er the ground,
And hear the low drum's muffled beating,
  With sad and most sorrowful sound,

While the notes of the fife and the bugle,
  With a wailing tone break on the air,
Proclaiming in numbers the saddest
  The bravest are sorrowing there.

'Tis sad and most plaintive of music,
  Its tones are most mournful to hear,
It tells us that one from our number
  Has ended his earthly career :
It tells us a brother has fallen,
  By disease or the hand of the foe,
And that there, with hearts saddened, brave com-
  Are laying his lifeless form low.   [rades

O, sad is the heart of the soldier,
  He grieves for a comrade laid low,
But hearts the most sad are those mourning,
  In the home which he left long ago ;
For there, in the home of the loving,
  Affliction's blows heaviest fall,
And tears of deep sorrow are stealing,
  From the eyes of the loving ones all.

O, sad aro these mournful death-dirges,
  That so often are heard in our land,
For they tell of the last earthly striving
  Of the bravest of liberty's band ;
But we'll turn not our hearts to despairing,
  Though amidst deep affliction and gloom,
For we've hope of a brighter day's dawning,
  When, to peace, war for aye yields his room.

TEARS FOR THE SOLDIER.

There are tears for the fallen soldier,
  Whose trials and labors are o'er,
For friends kind and loving are mourning
  In the home he returns to no more ;
Yes, though tearless may be the brave comrades
  Who bear him away to his grave,
Sad news has gone home to the loving,
  And their tears freely flow for the brave.

Oh ! war's worst affliction flies homeward,
  And pierces the warmest of hearts,
And in eyes that are not used to weeping, ·
  The tear-drops of sorrow it starts :
Loving sisters shed tears for a brother,
  The wife's for her fallen one flow,
And the silver-haired father and mother,
  In affliction and tears are bent low.

Yes, by all of the true and loving,
  In the home which he left long ago,
Tears of sorrow are shed for the fallen,
  For their hearts are all heaving with woe :
There are tears for the fallen soldier,
  Tears enough for to moisten his grave,
And hearts that grow weary with mourning
  Will ever remember the brave.

PARTY STRIFE.

Friends of freedom, raise your aims,
Rise above all party claims :
'Tis no time for party strife
When a dread foe seeks our life ;
Ours is work that should be done
As if all our aims were one,
And through each dark trial hour
We should move as one great power.

In our homes and council halls,
Freedom now on each one calls,
She has work for you and me,
She has work for all the free ;
There's a task for each assigned,
Both for muscle and for mind ;
Let us then, like freemen true,
Freedom's work in earnest do.

In our country's present plight
We should all see by one light,
And as one, where justice leads,
We should live in noble deeds ;
Then, whatever may betide,
Let us not our strength divide,
But together stand as one,
Till our country's work is done.

If divided now we be
Darker times our land will see,
For not far off treads our foe,
Working ruin, working woe,

Wasting precious human life,
In a most unholy strife;
Then, O Northmen! stand as one,
Till the work of war is done.

Ours is freedom's country yet:
Ours is toil for true hands set;
And as *one* in heart and mind
Union ties the north should bind:
Yes, while on the field of strife,
Men most brave guard freedom's life,
We together here should stand
As the home-guard of our land.

SELF-EXAMINATION.

'Tis the closing hour of evening:
   I have finished this day's task;
Now, concerning this day's labor,
   I myself these questions ask:

Have I added joy or sorrow
   To the sum of life to-day?
Have I walked the path of virtue,
   Or in sin's alluring way?

Have I sought my own heart's welfare,
   With a selfish aim alone?
Or have others been made better
   As the hours away have flown?

Have I cheered a heart desponding?
   Have I made earth's sorrow less?
Have the thoughts which I have uttered
   Taken wings to curse or bless?

Have I done unto all others
  As I'd have them do to me ?
Have my motives been as worthy
  As a Christian man's should be ?

Shall I on the coming morrow
  Do as I have done to-day ?
Or from this day's finished labor
  Have I learned a better way ?

It has been my soul's ambition
  All my work to do so well,
It should in the plainest language
  Of its own high merits tell.

But if I have erred in doing,
  From this morning till this eve,
May I of the coming morrow
  A far clearer record leave.

I would have the best improvement
  Mark the progress of my days,
Till my life's last golden sunset
  Lends to earth its twilight rays.

'Tis the closing hour of evening ;
  This day's work at last is done ;
Now I go to rest in quiet
  Till the morrow's rising sun.

INDEPENDENCE DAY.

This is our brightest day of story,
　　The day our fathers loved the best,
They who have won undying glory,
　　And gone to their long place of rest.
It is the bright and glorious day
　　When freedom to our land was born,
And earnest hearts resolved for aye
　　Oppression's power and pride to scorn.

We love this glorious day of story,
　　And it will ever sacred be,
To those who love our nation's glory,
　　And love the cause of liberty.
We love it as the dawn of time,
　　When freedom's grandest ship of state
Was launched upon a sea of crime
　　To work a revolution great.

Sweet day! blest day! bright day of story!
　　Our nation's day of jubilee!
May time dim not thy well-earned glory,
　　But make it dearer to the free!
Glide on, glide on, O years of time,
　　Shine on, O sun, in heaven's blue dome,
And while upon thy course sublime,
　　May this fair land be Freedom's home!

Yes, while time writes our future story
　　May this day still be loved the best,
And may it brighter grow in glory
　　Till all the world with freedom's blest—
Till all who now in bondage wait
Shall see oppression swept away,
And with the free, the good and great,
　　Enjoy an Independence day.

Each sun that lengthens out our story
   Looks down on graves where rest the brave,
And though it looks on soil most gory
   May it ne'er look on Freedom's grave,
But while a human heart shall beat,
   Oft as this glorious day comes round,
May freedom-loving hearts repeat
   Our cheering songs on this free ground.

THE MEN WE WANT.

We want more men who would serve their land
   With a far higher motive than gold :
We want them in every high station to stand,
And we want them for subjects of every band,
   From the days of their youth till they're old.

We want more men like Fremont in camp,
   And went them in vast numbers too,
To the voice of the bugle away to tramp
Over mountainous regions and marshlands damp,
   And the work of the soldier do.

We want more men who are strong and brave,
   Who their time and their talents would give,
To freedom restore to each downtrodden slave,
And stay the dread hand of each traitor and knave,
   That Freedom forever may live.

We want more men of a Washington stamp,
   Who care *more* for their county than pay :
We want them for council, we want them for camp,
And to wrest of his power each political scamp
   Who is working our ruin each day.

We want more men with ambition true,
  For the good of our nation to work;
And there's work enough for us all to do,
Work enough for mind and for muscle too,
  And from duty none justly can shirk.

We want more men who are true every way
  As the needle that points to the pole—
More men who care naught for vain pomp and display
Men who labor for justice and truth every day
  As if they possessed a true soul.

THE GOOD TIME COMING.

Progression's car is rolling on,
  The "good time" nearer bringing;
And earnest hearts to aid its dawn
  New songs of peace are singing.
'Tis coming up the steeps of Time,
  That blessed day ideal;
The day of all our dreams sublime
  Will surely yet be real.
        No hand can stay
        The coming day
Of which we've long been dreaming,
        For truths sublime,
        In reason's time,
Will real make life's seeming.

We may not live to see the day
  Of which we sing so cheering;
But down to earth it makes its way,
  And every day it's nearing.

O! brothers, bid that blest day speed,
  And all good omens cherish;
Show to the world, by word and deed,
  You mean no good shall perish.
        Yes, aid along,
        With speech and song,
  That day which long has tarried,
        That wrong and crime,
        In every clime,
  May to their graves be carried.

As was foretold in days of old,
  When lived the ancient sages,
'Tis speeding on with bearing bold
  To bless the world for ages:
'Tis forward speeding, day and night,
  As fate at first decreed it,
And if we all would *try* we might
  Still faster onward speed it.
        O! who would stay
        The coming day
  Which so much joy presages?
        Who would not live,
        And life's toil give,
  To bring those blissful ages?

The world's best age is yet in store:
  The good time sure is coming:
We hear it in the cannon's roar!
  We hear it in the drumming!
We hear it where our brave boys shout
  Upon the field of battle!
We hear it plain, too plain to doubt,
  Where shot and shell now rattle!

It comes, though slow,
Through wail and woe,
Cheered on by tongues and presses!
It comes, though late,
Through trials great,
As Truth's great cause progresses.

Yes that most blissful time draws near,
To end this world's afflictions;
And when all men life's laws revere,
Fulfilled are these convictions:
Mankind will form one brotherhood,
The reign of war be over,
The wife and children will be good,
The husband be a lover:
We'll kindly speak,
And always seek
The welfare of each other:
Each one we see
Will truly be
A sister or a brother.

Mankind will then so love true worth
That every man and woman,
Will spend a lifetime here on earth
As though divinely human.
The days of life, from youth to age,
Will be serenely pleasant,
And man will pass from stage to stage
Enjoying all the present.

Then strive alway
To bring the day
Of which we've long been dreaming ;
Join hearts and hands,
Throughout all lands,
And real make life's seeming.

Press on, press on, my brother man,
  The whole world needs reforming !
Live up to wisdom's noblest plan,
  And Error's forts keep storming.
Say not this is another's work,
  'Tis yours and every other's,
For Heaven designed no man to shirk
  Where all should live like brothers.
      Then add your mite
      To aid the right
And bring the good time nearer ;
      Enlighten mind
      Till all mankind
Their way of life see clearer.

The Past is like a field of blood,
  As written out in story,
The Future, like a rising flood,
  In hope is bright with glory ;
And when we all learn Wisdom's way,
  And in true faith grow stronger,
Truth's day will dawn, and Wrong, for aye,
  Oppress the world no longer.

Then live in hope,
With Error cope,
And cherish the ideal,
Till all on earth
Live lives of worth,
And our best dreams are real.

THE CHRISTIAN'S PETITION.

Great Creator, God, Jehovah,
Thou who art the world's great mover,
Thou who reignst all things over,
  Guide us with thy holy hand:
In our days of deep privation,
Hear our earnest invocation,
And extend sweet consolation
  To the worthy of our land.

Bless the soul that others blesses,
Bless the hand that none oppresses,
Bless him who no law transgresses
  And forever keep him pure.
Be his toil in war-fields gory,
Or where Peace doth tell her story,
If he seeks good more than glory
  Give him life that will endure.

In all fields of labor holy,
Where the work goes on too slowly,
Cheer the toilers, howe'er lowly,
  And their faith in good increase:
Teach their spirits perseverance,
Show that more than in appearance
Duty is the only clearance
  Which secures the soul true peace.

Let no Judas' hand betray us,
'Gainst the good let none array us,
For eternal blessings pay us
   For the good we do in time.
Out of deepest tribulation,
With our freedom's preservation,
To a glorious destination,
   Lead us on life's way sublime!

Great Creator, God, Jehovah,
Thou who art the world's great mover,
Thou who reignest all things over,
   Guide us o'er the sea of time:
Guide us in the work before us,
Till our triumph song and chorus
Echo in the high heavens o'er us
   With a most soul-thrilling chime!

THE DRUNKARD'S HOME.

AIR.—*Old Folks at Home.*

There is a drunkard's dwelling lowly,
     Not far away,
Where lives a mother pure and holy
     In sorrow every day.
There in that home where love was plighted,
     In days gone by,
Her youthful hopes have all been blighted,
     And now she longs to die:
She is very sad and lonely,
     And her tears oft flow,
For her sad heart is freighted only
     With a wearying weight of woe.

What are the feelings of that mother,
   Toil-worn and sad,
Without a sister, friend or brother,
   Her weary soul to glad,
As almost hopelessly she's musing
   On days by-gone—
On memory's freighted ocean cruising
   Where joy and peace have flown?
They can never be related;
   We can never know
How heavily her heart is freighted,
   With a wearying weight of woe.

Gaze on the loved ones she is tending
   In her sad home,
While their father his time is spending
   Where licensed men sell rum:
Know once a father fond caressed them,
   In childish play:
Know once a father truly blessed them
   As fathers only may:
Know they dwelt there joyous-hearted,
   Ere the rum-fiend came,
And from a heart most loving parted
   The pure sunlight of love's flame.

Yes, once they dwelt a happy number
   As e'er was found,
Each day brought joy, each night sweet slumber,
   And gaily time rolled round.
The fairest flowers the earth adorning
   Then bloomed for them,

But, oh! at last there came a morning
    When each dropped from its stem;
And as those bright flowers perished,
    There before their gaze,
So died the hopes that mother cherished
    In her youth's most joyous days.

Their summer-time no more brings plenty
    For winter's store,
So each day's portion is so scanty
    They often sigh for more;
But there's for them no well-filled measure
    When cold winds blow,
For, though the rich are near with treasure,
    No charity they show.
Ah! so wretched, sad and lonely
    Is that mother there,
Upon her face are traces only
    Of the deepest grief and care.

And though she knew a time most pleasant,
    Bright, bright with bloom,
The unknown future and the present
    Are mantled deep in gloom;
And now that mother low is kneeling,
    Bowed down in prayer;
To all true hearts she is appealing,
    Though none are near her there;
And the prayer which she now offers
    Tells of earth's vain show—
Tells how each day of life she suffers
    In this world of want and woe.

She kindly asks to be protected
From rum's dread power.
She kindly asks to be directed
Through each dark trial hour.
Thus earnestly she there is pleading
A martyr's cause,
Thus earnestly she's interceding
For better, nobler laws;
Still the cold world round her heedeth
Not her sad heart's prayer,
But, knowing what the wronged heart needeth
Leaves her in deep sorrow there.

And for the dearly loved ones round her,
Too sad to play,
With all the hope with which God crowned her
That mother now doth pray;
But memory takes her back to others,
Of long ago—
To parents, sisters and fond brothers,
And tears of sorrow flow.
Oh! her heart is sad and weary—
Of a life joy-riven:
She longeth for a home less dreary—
Longeth for a home in Heaven.

A Soldiers Meditations on the Eve of Battle.

Lonely by my camp-fire lying,
Gazing at the embers dying,
Thoughts and fancies throng my being
As they never did before:
Backward through the past I wander,
On most trying scenes I ponder,

And most earnestly I wonder
  What the future has in store—
What of good and what of evil
  What the great future has in store
  For mankind the wide world o'er.

Darkness over all things hovers,
Pall-like land and sea it covers,
And all nature's wrapt in silence
  As it oft has been before :
Not a sound disturbs the slumber
Of the vast reposing number
Which this care-worn world encumber—
  All is silence—nothing more!
Weary souls are sweetly sleeping
  Who will waken soon once more
  When these dark night hours pass o'er.

Round me here are soldiers lying
By their camp-fires slowly dying,
And perchance they're sweetly dreaming
  Of most happy days in store ;
It may be that friends the dearest—
Friends the warmest and sincerest—
Friends they e'er will keep the nearest
  Tread with them their homestead floor—
Tread with them in joyous dreaming
  That oft trodden homestead floor
  Where perchance they'll tread no more.

Oh! how swiftly time is flying
To the vast throngs round me lying,
As if through the long, long future
  Blessings were for all in store!

Sleep, sweet sleep, thus oft we take it,
Take it and again forsake it—
Would we never more might break it
　To pursue war's work once more!
But when comes the morning sunlight
　Martial strains will sound once more—
　All this silence will be o'er.

Yes, as soon as dawns the morrow,
Which should bring to none a sorrow,
Here where all is rest and quiet
　Jarring sounds will ring once more:
Men will form in line of battle,
Deadly shot and shell will rattle,
Men will fall like slaughtered cattle,
　'Midst the battle's awful roar!
Wildest strains of martial music
　Mingling with the cannon's roar
　All this silence will be o'er!

Soldiers wounded, dead and dying,
On the cold ground will be lying
Mangled forms most grim and ghastly,
　Covered with their own heart's gore!
Yes, as we have here predicted,
Man by man will be afflicted
Worse than pen hath e'er depicted,
　And in just a few hours more;
For on battle ground are resting
　Armies that will strive once more,
　And their work will soon be o'er!

Then the news will go to mothers,
Loving sisters and fond brothers,

Age-crowned fathers and all others
  Who the Union would restore ;
And while flow their tears of sorrow,
They will consolation borrow,
Thinking that their country's morrow
  Will be brighter evermore
For their brave and noble striving—
  Yes, seem brighter evermore
  For the precious blood they pour.

What a scene for contemplation
In a young and growing nation !—
What will be is for your guessing,
  Or to read of when 'tis o'er,
For I now essay to mention
Things which need the world's attention,
Which will prove a sure prevention
  Of dread scenes on days in store,
In the future which is holding
  All of time we have in store,
  Be it one brief day or more.

O, that we could shun disaster !
Would that we could error master
Without using deadly weapons
  Such as stain our land with gore !
Then would surely dawn that morning
Of which man hath had forewarning
When earth's children, error scorning,
  Good will seek and nothing more—
When all men shall be contented
  With what's needed and no more,
  Much or little be the store.

But the world is dark with sorrow,
Clouds portend a dark to-morrow,
There are men who will not reason
  Thirsting after human gore !
Shall the righteous by them perish ?
Must those fall who virtue cherish ?
Shall *good less* than evil flourish
  Through all years of time in store ?
No ; there is a glorious future—
  There's a time for Truth in store,
  And she'll reign the whole world o'er.

Truth, whose light is pure and holy,
Moves the high and moves the lowly,
Moves the whole world forward slowly,
  Opening wider Reason's door :
Truth is all the world's physician,
She has clear, far-seeing vision,
And in perfectest condition
  All man needs she has in store :
For the world's great wrongs o'ercoming,
  She has precious light in store
  Which will brighten evermore.

By Truth's light wrongs will be righted,
Hearts and homes and temples lighted,
Till to close investigation
  None will bar up Reason's door :
All should trust to agitation,
Earnest thought and contemplation,
Knowing that investigation
  Yields of truth the richest store—
Yields us knowledge, light and wisdom,
  Which true souls delight to store
  For free usage evermore !

Each should learn to be consistent—
Toil to make that day less distant,
When all men with holy motives
　　Use kind words to close Wrong's door .
Reasoning words alone are needed
To set right what has preceded.
And if these could be well heeded
　　Blood would stain this earth no more :
Man would use for righting troubles
　　Reasoning words and nothing more—
　　Harsher strife would all be o'er.

He who will not trust his reason,
Wrong to right at every season,
Surely is a moral coward—
　　Moral coward—nothing more :
Force alone is his correction,
Force alone is his protection,
He knows nothing of reflection
　　For he's closed up Reason's door ;
And he'll use war-weapons only
　　Till he opens Reason's door,
　　And of truth obtains a store.

Let us then be up and doing
In the field we've been reviewing,
And with deeds of love and kindness
　　Peace throughout the world restore ;
Yes, with holiest ambition,
Let us change the world's condition
Aiding Truth, the great Physician,

Doing good and nothing more:
Truth will work out man's redemption:
Let us aid her evermore—
Aid her till life's toils are o'er.

Let us view all things created,
And as we're to all related,
Let us with most high ambition
All life's mysteries explore:
Let us learn by meditation—
Learn by calm investigation—
Learn man's highest destination,
And our faith increase still more:
Faith will go beyond our seeing
When of things we've knowledge more,
For with knowledge Faith can soar.

Aid our country, fathers, mothers;
Aid our country, sisters, brothers,
Till the light of Truth and Reason
Bars for aye Oppression's door:
Care for more than vain earth-glory
Which may written be in story,
When this reign of war most gory
Shall be past forevermore:
Care for all that's worth preserving—
All that's good and nothing more,
Much or little be the store.

Yes, toil on, O brothers, ever,
Labor on with high endeavor,
And with light that is divinest
This fair land to peace restore:

Guard our country through all dangers,
Guard Guerrilla raiding rangers:—
Freedom's foes to truth are strangers
   Needing light and nothing more—
Needing light from Truth's clear fountains—
  Truth's clear light and nothing more,
  Pure as from Heaven's radiant shore.

Oh! look up time-toilers, ever;
Upward look with high endeavor,
And from Truth's divinest fountains
   Aim to make your soul's whole store:
Be your spirits howe'er lowly,
Striving with a purpose holy,
You can rise though it be slowly,
  And in time to proud heights soar;
Yes, to heights that are divinest,
  With high purpose you can soar
  To be lowered nevermore.

At each stage of life and season
Right earth's wrongs with truth and reason,
And in souls that lack true wisdom
   Light from Truth's clear fountains pour:
Let this moral reformation
Spread through every clime and nation,
To both high and low in station,
  And war's reign will soon be o'er,
Swords will be laid down in earnest,
  By mankind the whole world o'er—
  To be lifted—nevermore!

RECONCILIATION.

When we differ from another
  Whom we think to rashly err,
We shall ever act most wisely
  Kindly with him to confer.

Friendly interchange of feeling
  Fills no human heart with guile,
But with men of worthy motives
  It will all hearts reconcile.

Friendly words can win to friendship
  Hearts that are most cold with hate,
For where threats can never enter,
  Friendly words can penetrate.

Threats avail mankind but little ;
  Harsh words grate upon the ear ;
Words of sympathy and kindness
  Mortals soonest bend to hear.

Yes, all words with coldness spoken
  Further set our souls apart,
While the words that glow with friends
  Bring us nearer, heart to heart.

Then remember, ye who differ,
  Ye whose hearts are filled with guile,
Friendly interchange of feelings
  Always tends to reconcile.